KEITH THOMAS WALKER

POOR RIGHTEOUS POET

KEITH THOMAS WALKER

KEITHWALKERBOOKS, INC
This is a UMS production

POOR RIGHTEOUS POET

KEITHWALKERBOOKS

Publishing Company
KeithWalkerBooks, Inc.
P.O. Box 331585
Fort Worth, TX 76163

All rights reserved. Except for use in any review, the reproduction or utilization of this manuscript in whole or partial in any form by any mechanical, electronic, or other means, not known or hereafter invented, including photocopying, xerography, and recording, or in any information retrieval or storage system, is forbidden without written permission of the publisher, KeithWalkerBooks, Inc.

For information write
KeithWalkerBooks, Inc.
P.O. Box 331585
Fort Worth, TX 76163

All characters in this book have no existence outside the imagination of the author and have no relation whatsoever to anyone bearing the same name or names. They are not even distantly inspired by any individual known or unknown to the author and all incidents are pure invention.

Copyright © 2013 Keith Thomas Walker

ISBN-13 DIGIT: 978-0-9850500-7-8
ISBN-10 DIGIT: 0985050071
Library of Congress Control Number: 2013916843
Manufactured in the United States of America

First Edition

Visit us at www.keithwalkerbooks.com

KEITH THOMAS WALKER

Poetry doesn't sell well – yes, I knew that before I published this book. So this is dedicated to you, the reader, who purchased this collection. I pray that you'll always enjoy literature as much as I do.

This book means a lot to me. I never talk about some of the things I'm bold enough to present in poetic form.

Oh, and I have a YouTube channel. I recite a lot of poetry on YouTube, most of which is also in this collection. If YouTube is still a thing, by the time you read this, you can watch me perform some of this poetry online. My channel is KeithWalkerBooks. If you have trouble finding it, simply type "keithwalkerbooks" (with no spaces) in the YouTube search bar, and it should pull up my videos.

Happy Reading!

MORE BOOKS BY KEITH THOMAS WALKER

Fixin' Tyrone
How to Kill Your Husband
A Good Dude
Riding the Corporate Ladder
The Finley Sisters' Oath of Romance
Blow by Blow
Jewell and the Dapper Dan
Harlot
Plan C (And More KWB Shorts)
Dripping Chocolate
The Realest Ever
Jackson Memorial

Novellas

Might be Bi Part One
Harder

Visit keithwalkerbooks.com for information about these and upcoming titles from KeithWalkerBooks

ACKNOWLEGMENTS

Of course I would like to thank God, first and foremost, for giving me the creativity and drive to pursue my dreams and the understanding that I am nothing without Him. I would like to thank my wife for being my first and most important critic, and I would like to thank my mother for always pushing me to be the best I can be. I would like to thank Janae Hampton for being the best advisor, supporter and little sister a brother could ever have. I would also like to thank (in no particular order) Jason Owens, Brandy Rees, Denise Bolds, Sabrina Scott, Dianne Guinn, Kierra Pease, Sharon Blount, BRAB Book Club, Trey Williams and Uncle Steven Thomas, one love. I'd like to thank everyone who purchased and enjoyed one of my books. Everything I do has always been to please you. I know there are folks who mean the world to me that I'm failing to mention. I apologize ahead of time. Rest assured I'm grateful for everything you've done for me!

TABLE OF CONTENTS

PART ONE
HODGE PODGE

Page 11. Emmett Till
Page 13. A Jacked up World
Page 14. The Circus
Page 15. A Lion and an African
Page 17. All Hallow's Eve
Page 18. April
Page 18. California Dreaming
Page 19. Cornucopia
Page 21. Moonlit Chores
Page 24. Monster in my Room
Page 24. Springtime
Page 25. TDC
Page 25. An Unidentified Object Flying
Page 28. Obama

PART TWO
LOVE CONQUERS ALL

Page 32. If I Could Sing
Page 34. Cum
Page 34. Blue Reflections
Page 35. Forever
Page 35. Unbridled
Page 36. You and I
Page 36. You're Gone

Page 37. Your Loveliness
Page 37. Perfect Passion Unfulfilled
Page 38. My Star
Page 39. Goddess
Page 40. This Thing
Page 41. Fire Follows Moon
Page 41. I Love You!
Page 42. Perchance a Dream
Page 43. Sweet Divine
Page 43. Wondrous Vision
Page 44. Jasmine
Page 44. The Beauty of You

PART THREE
ROCK BOTTOM

Page 46. Wasted
Page 47. Those Who Practice Dealing
Page 47. Rock Bottom
Page 48. The Big League
Page 51. Soiled Doves
Page 51. My Sorry for 2004
Page 52. Da Crack Poem
Page 56. Backsliding Brothers
Page 56. Addiction
Page 57. Big H
Page 57. Whispers
Page 58. Missing Babies
Page 59. He Has Them
Page 60. Dream
Page 60. For Mama
Page 61. The Overdose

PART FOUR
A HIGHER POWER

Page 62. I Adore You
Page 63. God's Response to Job
Page 63. Enemy's Camp
Page 64. Before I Lay me Down to Sleep
Page 64. Drizzles
Page 65. Loneliness
Page 66. Matthew 6:6
Page 66. Be Lord
Page 66. Burdens Down
Page 67. Lamb of God
Page 68. Let it Rain
Page 69. Acid Rain
Page 69. Romans 7 & 8
Page 70. Trapped
Page 71. Demons: My Testimony

PART FIVE
STOP! THE VIOLENCE

Page 74. I'll Take Your Blood
Page 75. A Bullet and a Knuckle
Page 78. Colored Rags
Page 79. Dulce et Decorum
Page 80. A Place for Me
Page 81. Badass
Page 82. Drip Drop
Page 84. Crime Caucuses
Page 85. Filthy
Page 86. Innocent
Page 87. The First 48
Page 91. The Killing Field
Page 92. What is Black?

Page 92. Put Down Your Guns
Page 94. Mansfield County Jail
Page 95. All For Me
Page 96. Black Hate
Page 96. Stick in the Mud
Page 97. Can't Stop Won't Stop

PART SIX
IT'S OKAY TO LAUGH

Page 99. Lately
Page 100. Dope Ray Me
Page 100. Menace in the Sky
Page 102. The Killer's Knife
Page 102. Possum
Page 103. Different Chokes
Page 104. These Bars
Page 105. Texas Hell
Page 106. The Poisoned Punch
Page 106. If Deer Had Guns
Page 107. If She Delights You
Page 108. Those Were the Days
Page 108. Snot Dragons
Page 109. Y'all Niggas Tripping
Page 110. You're Black Too

POOR RIGHTEOUS POET

PART ONE

HODGE
PODGE

Emmett Till

His name was Emmett Till
And I remember that name
I remember it more than the name of the white man
Who wrapped that barbed-wire around that cotton gin fan
Or the black man
Who was the first in Mississippi to take the stand
And point a gnarled, black finger at a white man
And accuse him of murder
I remember Emmett Till
And I remember that day he had to learn some
Down-home, southern ways
Those smart remarks he was dared to say
See, Emmett spoke to white girls back home everyday
But there were glitches in the north/south traditions
And those good ole boys felt the need to
Hitch up their britches
And honor their southern bitches

POOR RIGHTEOUS POET

They put together a lynching party
And they went hard
Drove right up to Emmett's uncle's house and parked
Excuse me, partner
But we're looking for the boy with the smart remarks
At the store earlier today
'Cause we gon' make him pay
And that's what they did
They walked right in
And drug Emmett out with screams and kicks
They threw him in a truck
And took him to a barn
And roughed him up
And swolled him up
And split his wig
They cut off his tongue
And cut off his dick
They fucked him up
And axed him up
And shot him up
And wrapped his throat up
With barbed wire
And tied the other end to a heavy fan
They threw Emmett in a creek
And watched him sink
They called Emmett a creep as his blood seeped
I remember his name
I remember it more than the name of the white judge
And all white jury
Who had eye witness testimony
But still
They let those good ole boys go

They let them go to let the whole world know
That if you're from up north
And you mosey on down a little ways
And happen upon some of these here country folks
You best watch your mouth
'Cause down in Miss'sippi, they like to hitch up their britches
And honor their southern bitches
And when they brought Emmett back
Up north
The blacks and whites were all waiting
At the train station
And Emmett's mom ordered that casket open wide
To show the whole world southern pride
And what was inside
My God, that face, those eyes
Is that the Elephant Man or a fourteen year old child?
A child who had the nerve to whistle
At a white woman
To say, "Hey, baby"
To a white woman
Emmett's mom showed the whole world
What they did to her baby
So I can't forget Emmett's name
Or what happened to him
On that blistering Mississippi weekend

A Jacked up World

If all jailbirds were simply freed
Rapists, killers and petty thieves
Free to ravage and loot the streets

POOR RIGHTEOUS POET

And blessed with an immunity
From prosecution and police
The world would be jacked up, I think

If all birds left the heights and trees
And came with bats and frogs and bees
And snakes and lions roamed the streets
As free as God meant them to be
If creatures took back society
The world would be jacked up, I think

If somebody shot Kennedy and King
And AIDS became a BLACK PEOPLE disease
And crack broke poor families by degrees
And jihadist crashed planes into Wall Street
And no one read a book, too stuck on TV
The world would be jacked up, I think

The Circus

Sitting in a gazebo
Watching the wind blow slow and sweet
Like infant sneezes
Leaves caught on soft breezes
Are as soft as feathers
Hot caramel scents
Hover like hummingbirds
And water the tongues of children
Who smile with toothy grins
Free from sin
They cling to their mother's dresses

And they are precious
And they are blessed
And cotton candy is swirled
Into huge pink and blue clouds
It electrifies the crowd that gathers 'round
The sounds of games and fun
Are on one mind and one accord
Though scattered and diverse
The ringmaster gets everyone's attention
As the elephants make their grand entrance
With their trunks high
And their saddles shine with glitter
And the girls that are lifted by the beasts
Are as light as whispers
And everyone litters, but no one is reprimanded
No one is demanding
Young lovers hold hands
As they streak for the rides
The Ferris wheel that takes them high
So high that no one can see them and insist
That they stop
When they kiss
It's like fireworks
In their minds
That makes them blind

A LION AND AN AFRICAN

The sun, fierce and brutal pounds down hard on the African plains
The land is dry and dusty, through this season without rain

POOR RIGHTEOUS POET

I look back to spy my guest, who stepped so boldly as he came
The lean African follows brazenly on this blistering African plain

His name is Ungala, and I've caught his scent before
On dark nights when his persistence chilled my being to the core
His dark skin is sun-beaten, his palms and feet a lighter tan
There is cunning in his eyes and a sharp blade in his hand
I know he wants to take my hide back to his home to be a man

My prized and precious hide, with its long and cherished mane
A symbol, well respected on these deadly African plains
It protects me when I lurk among the sharp and prickly leaves
It stands erect and threatening, when I growl and bear my teeth
I turn and face Ungala. The African stops and stares at me

This boy, this adolescent, is almost half-crazed in his plan
Determination brought him to me. He will not leave with empty hands
The grisly paint he wears is now an almost frightening stain
His eyes – emotionless – reflect no fear, hesitance or pain
So we stand, ten feet apart, on this fiery African plain

I force myself not to lunge and rip his belly with my claws
And feed on his sweet flesh before his body begins to fall
I ease open my mouth to show the boy my feline fangs

And let out a warning growl to add excitement to this game
His grip on the sword tightens, but his expression does not change

Suddenly a fury rose in me. My aggression had no bounds
I was already in the air before I knew my paws had left the ground
I clamp my teeth into his throat, open my mouth and bite again
His blade slips between my ribs and pierces my precious heart within

Now as I lay on top of him, I feel the first swollen drops of rain
As the sun fades from the sky on this cool African plain

All Hallow's Eve

Geckos and wriggling, slithering lizards
Gooey eyeballs, toad innards, chicken livers and gizzards
Crushed snails with rat tails, cat droppings and worms
Boiled together with vulture feathers and other creepies that squirm
'Tis the season for witches to cruise brooms and stir brews
And cast spells that spell doom, leaving Christians confused
When green gremlins and hobgoblins concoct fiendish folly
Teddy bears brandish spears, and girls flee from their dollies
Vampires in black dress seek to suck blood-filled necks
Tonight evil will not rest, so it really is best
To stay home! Bolt the doors! The dead brandish machetes
From their heads leak remains of their brains like spaghetti

There are no treats, only tricks, tom cats spit, grown men scream
Only nightmares, no sweet dreams on this foul Halloween!

April

Set adrift on memories blissful
Fragrant whispers, smooth and wistful
Scents of jasmine, shimmering waves
Of violet fields, golden sunrays
So comforting, a monarch rests
Softly a feather comes to rest
Gently, melodic happiness
Is streaming. Surely April's blessed

California Dreaming

It's cool under palm trees
At three o'clock in the afternoon
Soft breezes
That smell like the ocean
Caress my face
This place is addictive
The sights
The smells
The moon-driven waves
That lick the shore
In this place
Where it never rains
And it never snows
And girls have full hips

And thick thighs
And asses that won't
Stop
The mountains
So tall
And fresh
Refreshed and blessed
I'm reckless in my pursuit
Of sandy shores
Stunning sights
Delectable aromas that
Flow in color like a rainbow in my mind
As I close my eyes
And wish I wasn't leaving
Wish I lived here
Already fiending
California dreaming

Cornucopia

Outside it's brown and orange
Footballs storm through field goals
Little ones storm, too
Through crowded living rooms
Where kindred greet
And seek hugs and polite kisses
Have you met Lester?
This is the missus
See the bliss on aging faces
The warm embraces
Each takes a place

POOR RIGHTEOUS POET

And waits to taste
The ham
The duck
And Grandma's dressing
Looks the best
Salivating tongues bless the meal
The young ones too say grace
And lick their lips
Here come the plates!
So packed
So overwhelmed with food
That touches
And blends
The smell fills the room
The smiles do, too
And eager spoons
Dig into sweet potatoes
And mashed potatoes
And *Ooh*
Have you tasted the gravy?
No, I'm dieting. Well, maybe
Just a little
A little more
Oh, just turn it up and pour!
This Thanksgiving is for loving
Not just the food
But the matriarchs
The babies
Grandpa and God, too

Moonlit Chores
(Tribute to Edgar Allan Poe)

Once upon a midnight dreary
As I traversed a grassy clearing
My destination, no adventure, simply a visit to the store
As I walked, soon I stopped puzzled
I could have sworn I heard a *rustle*
I stopped dead and tensed each muscle
For some reason, ready for war
'Tis my imagination, I muttered, and continued to the store
My imagination, nothing more

I marched on, my tension leaving
This simple task of bread retrieving
Is a task I've never dreaded the many times I've gone before
But as the clearing became forest
And the night began its chorus
I became less and less joyous
About continuing this chore
What is it, I wondered, *chilling my being to the core?*
Yet I stepped onwards, towards the store

Out of the brush, there stepped a stranger
Quickly, 'fore I could summon danger
With Godspeed, he was upon me, flashing the toothy grin he wore
His dark eyes had all the fire
Of a demon's flaming pyre
I could scarcely fight desire
To empty my bowels into my shorts

POOR RIGHTEOUS POET

"You shouldn't be here," he muttered. *"God, I know,"* was my retort
"I was just going to the store"

Presently, his grin grew wider
As predators often conspire
I gasped a simple shriek, but if he heard it, he ignored
He wore a suit fit for a wedding
Totally contrary to the setting
Trimmed and crisp, he stood, forgetting
That grass and stinkweeds was his floor
"Do you see the moon?" he asked, his voice now deeper than before
"Yes," I said meekly, nothing more

The moon was full, which I'd expected
Known this, had I, before I checked it
And as my eyes came back to his, I was now filled with perfect horror
Because the man who did entreat me
Was now pained, with troubled breathing
And he *drooled*, a grown man teething
His drool fell on the suit he wore
I watched a moment longer, as teeth became fangs meant to gore
Then I fled through the darkened forest

Oh, my Dear Lord, I said to myself
I can't describe the fear that I felt
Even as I darted homewards, I heard a suit rip as it tore
Jesus, he's changing, this I knew
I sprinted faster, almost flew

But mere mortals only move
At a squirrels pace, maybe more
And the beast that pursued me was not the man whose suit had torn
"COME BACK!" His voice was now a roar

I looked back in time to peep
A darkened creature as it leaped
Talons or claws dug in me deeply – I was tackled to the floor
And it was there, beneath the moonlight
My blood flowed hot, I struggled to fight
I felt the fangs, then shock, then pure fright
As the beast selected my right arm
Beneath the biceps, tendons ripped, bones snapped hard as sinews tore
My arm was with me, never more

That was then, six months ago
Since then, springtime's given to snow
And as night falls, here I wander through this same enchanted forest
And though my wound has totally healed
Its nights like this I'm fully thrilled
Its nights like this I've fully killed
Hapless victims, some I adored
I truly pity any fool trekking through moonlight on a chore
For I am here, forever more

POOR RIGHTEOUS POET

Monster in my Room

There is a creature near my bed
He waits for me to show a leg
Or foot that he can quickly snatch
And climb aboard for a foul snack
Some think I mean the boogeyman
But I'm old enough to understand
That there's no creature like that, and
The monster in my room's a man
He sneaks in when I go to sleep
Sometimes he makes me take a peek
At his, *thing*, his private place
Sometimes he puts it in my face
He should be there, where Mommy lies
He shouldn't touch between my thighs
He shouldn't keep making me cry
He should be *dead*. I wish he'd die

Springtime

Sweet blissful breezes
Mother Nature's sneezes set adrift
Usher exotic tantrums of spring
Fountains of fragrances
Flowers awash
In an array of colors
A full spectrum
Exhausting the primary
Awaiting discovery
By attentive retina and pupils

Apt pupils of God's creation

TDC

Prisons cater to the elite
To keep the criminals off the streets
To give the upper class some peace
To control our society

The lock the black men up in jail
They put the Mexicans in hell
Poor whites can't afford their bail
All locked up in those crowded cells

But what of all the money lost?
How much do all these prisons cost?
How many young men's lives are tossed?
The whole system is default

Why not put money in the streets
To teach the kids, employ the thieves
To heal the drug addicted fiends
To restore our society?

An Unidentified Object Flying

Sleeping in a '72 pickup
A few hours past dusk
With dust from the barren landscape
Caking up around my tires
I desired another drink

POOR RIGHTEOUS POET

But as my eyelids drooped
On the brink of total collapse
And my face sagged like an unhappy clown mask
I thought better of it
My existence was already bleak
Far from the neat salesman who knocked on doors
Of pretty housewives
Some of them pleasant, some bitches
Far from neat, my whiskey was gone
And the stench on me was strong
And the list of my many failures was long
As long as my list of regrets
I longed for death
Yet God delivered more breaths
It was then that it came
As suddenly as rain on the fiery plains of Africa
It came
This thing
It was huge
With dull yellow and purplish lights
That sparkled all around me
The lights comforted me, in a strange way
I was at peace
Though this thing that hovered above me
Was the size of a football stadium
It was somehow floating
Less than half a mile above me
An unidentified object flying
With bright lights that bore through the hood of my truck
They shined on me
They were eyeing me
Spying on me

The contents of my briefcase
The dark places
Even the stains of liquor I wasted on the floorboard
Were examined
And then came the faces
Unlike any of the races I've ever seen
Definitely not from any of the places God made on this earth
These faces were oblong
And pale
Alien faces without noses
Surrounding me
They astounded me
I thought they were peaceful, until they bound me
And removed me from my pickup
I was picked up
By unseen hands
And I drifted
With nary a jerk or unsteady motion
No doubt having illusions from the potions
I'd earlier consumed
I relaxed
And became transfixed on the lights
And the faces
But then came the lasers
And it was all of a sudden clear
That this was no illusion
Unknown instruments
With odder parts protruding from them
Were thrust into me
Painfully
The faces looked on
The pure insanity

Overwhelmed me
I was terrified
I screamed and begged them to release me
I realized these beings were my enemy
When my penis was taken from me
My kidney and spleen
I thought my heart was next
Instead
They took my head

Obama

(Written November 2010)

Let's hear it for the prez!
Yeah, look at you dead heads
With your hands in your lap
Was doing a lot of yipping and yapping in 2008
'Cause back then, everybody was on *one* side of the line
When somebody said *Obama!*
You either loved him, or you hated him
But now we got these people in between
In between the ones calling him a nigger
And the ones who thought his inaugural address
Was as monumental as *I Have a Dream*
I'm talking about the ones
Who cast their ballot for Obama in 2008
'Cause they wanted to get us out the Bushes
Like Jesse Jackson
But now these same people wanna cut Obama's nuts off
Like Jesse Jackson
Because unemployment is rising

The banks are foreclosing
And the economy's steadily oozing down the drain
And Rush Limbaugh's on the radio
Telling you the Democrats are to blame

I'm sitting back, watching
And I'm wondering if America
Has been shooting up with Demerol
'Cause some of you are acting like you been in a coma
For the last five years
And you just woke up and realized America's messed up
And you looked up at the White House
And saw Obama holding the reigns
And when it comes to the blame game
You know it don't get no better
Than when there's a big, wide nose
And a smiling, black face
Behind the reigns

But I'm not going to harp on the fact
That a lot of my president's opponents are racist
Because ninety-nine percent of the ones
Who venerate James Earl Ray
Will deny it every time
Even though I read your posts and your blogs
And your comments on YouTube
And I saw the video on YouTube
Of the eight year old angel
At the McCain rally
The one who held her father's hand
And looked right at the camera and said
A monkey can't be president

POOR RIGHTEOUS POET

And her whole family laughed
Because she was as cute as a button
And I had to laugh, too
'Cause you said you wouldn't stoop
To racism and bigotry
Nuh-uh. Of course not. Not you
Fine
Get your David Duke looking-ass back in the closet
'Cause I'm not even talking to you

My beef is with the ones who cast the *right vote* in 2008
But in 2010, they thinking it's time for another change
I'm talking about the ones who stood to be counted
When he told us *"Yes I can!"*
But you didn't take a stand a year later
When parents plucked their kids from school
So they wouldn't hear the president's education speech
You didn't take a stand when Sarah Palin hit the tour circuit
And the tea party sprouted and grew
And Glen Beck promised America gloom and doom
You sat back and listened to the smears and the lies
When they questioned his citizenship
And found a way to demonize
Something as beautiful as *health care* for *everybody*
You sat idly by
When they told you Obama was setting up death panels
That would decide when your granny lived and died
You sat idly by

And I can't complain too much, 'cause I sat idly by, too
But tonight I'm pulling out my soap box
And I'm yelling from my stoop

And I'm taking a stand – like you should
But I don't care if you do
Sarah Palin is an idiot!
Rush Limbaugh's a liar!
Glenn Beck is a fear monger!
And McCain needs to retire
And fuck you, America, for feeding my president to the lions!
I got Obama's back!
I'm down like four flat tires

PART TWO

LOVE
CONQUERS ALL

IF I COULD SING

When a man loves a woman
Sugar pie, honey bun
You got me saying my, my, my
If I could, I would write a love song like that for you
I would get you in the mood like Luther Vandross
Show you some sensitivity, like Ralph Tresvant
Get freaky with you like Silk
Girl, I would drink you like milk
Make your panties steam
Melt you like ice cream
Damn, baby, I wish I could sing

I would write a love song
To show you all my fire and desire
I know you been high, girl
But I can take you higher

I'm inspired by your ebony eyes
The way you purse your lips
Those thick hips, juicy thighs
Jesus Christ!
Come and take me, baby!
I will yield to your will
I'll pay your telephone and automo–bills
No-Diggity
I wanna show you real love, like Mary J Blige
Or we can creep, like T-Boz and Left Eye
I see you telling me no, no, no
But I ain't too proud to beg, ma
I'll get down on bended knee
I will get down wherever and whenever you please
'Cause I wanna be down like Moesha
I'll treat you like a queen – Latifah
Tasha, Kim, Maria or Keisha
We need some U-N-I-T-Y
And I need your sweet apple pie
And if I could sing
I would write a rhyme so smooth, I would make the doves cry
And you'd be proud to tell your homegirls, *That boy is mine*
And you can ride my pony like Genuwine

Baby, if I could sing
I'd write a love song just for you
But I can't
So this love poem will just have to do

Cum

My God, this galactic wonder
Supreme physique. I long to plunder
To ravage – Ah, I've gone too far
Yet, light is ebbing. In this dark
The shadows make me bold. Your toes
Are cold. I kiss each one. Behold
Each kiss is higher than the one
Before. Each kiss gets to the point
Your scent – exotic taste, it's just
Too much, to touch, it's such a rush
So plush, your intersection is
This lust – this pleasure that you give
My will is yours. I yield. Just come
Here, let me show you, love. Just cum

Blue Reflections

What forces are these that make me see blue
Whenever I close my eyes?
A shade darker than deep sunset
A bit lighter than starlit skies
It captivates my body and controls my senses
Whenever my thoughts are of you
Its childlike simplicity makes it strangely complex
So weird and fantastically blue
It wraps my body like sweet perfumes
When I hold you in my arms
It captivates like budding tulips
It soothes like the break of dawn

I offer you a love so deep and so pure
And so undeniably true
You offer me a kiss from your sweet lips
And I'm immediately engulfed in blue

Forever

Sweet angel, your spirit so gently caresses
My essence. Your presence speaks softly. The nexus
Of my state of mind, sweet divine, you're the reason
For light, precious raindrops, the seasons. I believe in
True joy, for your kiss brings me happiness. Your smile
Warms my soul. Your touch births quick tremors. Sweet child
I entreat thee, I give you my dreams. My desires
Are yours as my heart is your captive. These fires
Burn deeply – completely ignited by you
I yearn for the moment to profess that, "I do"

Unbridled

Unbridled
Bound neither by rhythm nor rhyme
Climbing peaks of
Perfect passion
Ignited by
A kiss
Slow and sultry
Hot and anxious
Pleasing sensations
Sweet and sensual

Pulsating pleasure smothers quick gasps
Soft moans are
Consumed
By the moon
Light

You and I

Fire joins moon with dark eclipses
Shading portions of the earth
Distant stars collide without witness
Giving way to miraculous births
For each molecule a mate is provided
The seas burst forth as do the skies
Constantly entities are united
Then why not you and I?

You're Gone

Desolate regions of my mind
Where dark despair attempts to bind
And blind the joy that I once felt
On auburn evenings when I held
You close. Desire burned in heated
Passion. I'm yearning for the peaks
That smolder now. And as the streaks
Of tears come down. I feel uniquely
Pained. My heart pumps grief. You're gone
I'm stained. Dejected. Somehow alone
I grieve and pray for sweet relief
But none entreats. Alone I sleep

And think of you. It's then I find
Peace in the corners of my mind

Your Loveliness

Passionate rivulets cascade
Auburn hazes of sun sweet rays
Through fragrant jasmine scents I gaze
I'm awestruck by your loveliness

The forest painted. The autumn leaves
Crinkle beneath your steps. I breathe
But slightly, though my heartbeats peak
I'm smitten by your loveliness

Perchance to hold your hand in mine
I'm weakened by your pulse. Each time
You smile a tremor sweeps my spine
I praise God for your loveliness

Perfect Passion Unfulfilled

Perfect passion unfulfilled
Short-lived, quick thrills, now longing fills
My soul, wrought with clinging despair
Your smile, those eyes, simply not there
This nightmare endures outside sleep
Meekly, through bloodshot eyes I seek
Refuge, a love to take your place
I search in vain, for each embrace
Falls short. No substitute appears

No other love comes near. I fear
That with you all sunshine is gone
Away. I long to love. I moan
I'm wounded, girl. I simply want
You back. I want you to come home

My Star

Attempting to formulate the words
To express the pure depths of this
Unheard of joy
The elation I feel when you are close
This is real
What I feel is pure
It's marvelous
And you are so gorgeous
Not just in the physical
Your feats are mystical
Empirical
I'm engulfed
Engaged
In your eyes
I'm tossed
Each page I fill falls short
Of describing your glory
Each day I attempt to understand
This story
This fairy tale that has come to be
I know very well that it's you that makes me
Salivate
Captivated

I wait
For you to create in me a wave
Of ecstasy previously unknown
I count the minutes
When you leave me alone
Anticipation makes my love grow stronger
Until you return, and I long no longer
To hold you
And want you
And feel you
You are
My sunlight
A diamond
To me
A star

Goddess

Wondrous vision of beauty, so lovely
Sweet goddess, caress me, come bless me, come love me
And rub me. Yes, I'm feeling feisty, girl. Take me
Taste me. Make me want much more of you. Tasty
Each morsel is sweet like molasses. How sticky
Like honey, each drop keeps me licking. You're glistening
I'm listening. The rise and the fall of your heartbeats
They quicken. I can't sleep. I can't eat. I can't breathe
Feed me. Allow me to suckle. I can't speak
Need me as much as I need you, girl, intensely
Immensely, so wonderfully perfect. So lovely
Caress me. Come bless me, sweet thing. Come love me

This Thing

This thing
Like cosmos shifting in unseen galaxies
Galactic systems sliding
And colliding
Shaken
Breath-taking
Amazing visions of psychedelic waves of emotion
Natural wonders of this world, and beyond
And my tongue
Sometimes can't find words for this thing
This thing
That slides through crazed shades of red
And darker red
And circles about me
Enraptures me
And captures me
In those eyes
Shall I be bold and reveal that my
Soul
My being
My very essence quivers at the threshold of her gaze
Dazed
I waver between right and wrong
Crazed and sane
Bold and shamed
This thing has me
Straight-jacketed in a padded room
Confused
I pray for the sweet relief of her kiss

For the bliss
That only she gives
This thing is plotting
And it's got me
And it's love

Fire Follows Moon

Lathering up with bubbly bubbles
Slippery couples caress and couple
Naughty nymphos awake and spoon
As daybreak chastens sickly moon

Lighthearted lovers arm in arm
Find a spot both moist and warm
Juvenile delinquents eagerly consume
Themselves as bright sun chases moon

Unjust desires are righteously filled
With delicate passion as ecstasy spills
From one to another. Sexuality blooms
In twilight as fire follows moon

I Love You!

I'm ecstatic!
I'm a nut!
Watch me dance
And shake my butt!
Ain't got no butt
But so what!

POOR RIGHTEOUS POET

I love you and you love me!

I'm outrageous!
I'm too cool!
I'm contagious!
I'm a fool!
I can fly!
You know why?
'Cause I love you and you love me!

I'm unique!
I'm a geek!
I'm butt-naked!
I'm a freak!
You know why?
Fooled you this time
It's 'cause you're asleep
And you can't see me!

Perchance a Dream

Dark, despondent, desolate despair
Devours the passionate places where
We became one – when our desire
Peaked. But now the ancestral fires
Smolder beneath foul, putrid rains
Pained and hopeless loss now stains
That jasmine scent, those piercing eyes
The rancid regions of my mind
Are warped. Your precious love is gone
Your gentle touch is gone. I long

To have back golden coasts. The tides
Are stormy now. The breaks that rise
And drench me leave me soiled. The stream
Of love has passed, perchance a dream

Sweet Divine

(For Edmunds Valentine)

Winter breezes, crystal snowflakes
Cause rosy cheeks to adorn the face
Of her, my love, my heaven sent
Simplistic joy, my unrelenting
Source of warmth. Amazing light
Glows bright from her. Oh, if I might
Just touch – but I desire much
A kiss, those lips, so soft, it's just
A dream that keeps my poor heart throbbing
Longing to embrace her, stopping
Not with words. They can't express
My thoughts, this fear, my love. How blessed
I am. Amanda, sweet divine
How blessed I am to call her mine

Wondrous Vision

Wondrous vision of beauty glow
The light that radiates from you is wholly
Comforting. A gentle stream
Of passion flows from you. I dream
Of simple things. Your hand in mind
How lightening gently sweeps my spine

When our lips touch. How you entice me
With your eyes. I dream of nights
When we will flow as rivers. Streaming
Torrents are cascading, teaming
With desire. I hold my peace
Until we meet, when I release
This raging longing. Sweet lady, be mine
At least for now, beloved. Be mine

Jasmine

Precious like fairies, like diamonds, her eyes
Are like twilights that glisten, the sparkle – deprived
Of them, seasons crept slowly like sorrow. I withered
Like daisies not long for this world. Foul wizards
Sick demons that once intervened – now defied
By His glory, and she's here with me, and her eyes
Filled with love – focused keenly on me. Her laughter's
Like harp strings that drift from the heavens. I'd rather
Have her in my arms than all riches this world
Has to offer. None compare to my little girl

The Beauty of You

Roses are red, some are pink, others white
Violets come in purples and turquoise and blues
Your eyes shine as bright as a samurai's knife
Your glow – more radiant than any rainbows bright hues
Your character's untouchable, unrivaled, I'm dazed
Your beauty's unfaltering, incomparable, sans rules
A thousand great poets working thousands of days

Could not find the words for the beauty of you
Foreign flora blossom and flourish each day
Some dazzling, some emitting the sweetest perfumes
Even if perfect roses grew wild from this page
This wouldn't compare to the beauty of you
Exotic orchards could root and grow stems from this page
But this wouldn't come close to the beauty of you

PART THREE

ROCK
BOTTOM

Wasted

Alone without vision or moonlight. The dark
Is overwhelming. I'm cowering. I'm floundering. I'm stark
Naked. This place is beyond freezing. My shivering
Bones are Morse code, quickening. I'm withering
Away. I'm decaying. I'm rotting. I'm rotten
I'm blinded by the signs. All warnings forgotten
Thick cotton fills my veins. Down my neck drips dark stains
From my ears leak the liquefied remains of my brain
And I've gained no deep visions, only cell loss and fission
No keen insight. Division. There's pressure. There's tension
This calamity is passionately blameless. I'm tasteless
With each breath I taste death. I'm aimless. I'm wasted

Those who Practice Dealing

Dirty rotten scoundrels stealing
Backdoor burglarizing, pealing
Paint clean off the walls, 'cause healing
Comes from those who practice dealing
Death to those who're hooked. Appealing
Girls submit to constant drilling
Face down, ass up. That filthy feeling
Leaves when they meet those who're dealing
Death into the lives of squealing
Infants born in Sheol. Willing
Saps are caught up in the killing
Fields of those who practice dealing

Rock Bottom

The truth was right
Before my eyes
About my lies
And I despise
The tears I made
My children cry
And my wife cried
And Mama cried
Inside I knew
I compromised
My life, my mind
My peace, my pride
Doors locked – I hide
But I can't hide

POOR RIGHTEOUS POET

The pain that ripped
My soul, the price
Too high – Oh Christ
Dear God. Damn. Why?
Can't catch this bitch
This fix – this itch
This devil's dish
This mix. This shit
A Homeboy says give
My life to Christ
Maybe I'll try
Perhaps I might
Tonight

The Big League

One moonlit night
Warm skies
Moonshines
A parking lot's bright light shines
On you
As you stoop like a baboon
Got a hammer in your hand
Like a gremlin you creep
Too lowly to stand
Got your eyes on the prize
The windows at the Conoco
Built strong – Ford tough
But with a hammer in the hands
Of the fiend you turned out to be
With your heart and your mind stammering

Those windows won't hold
Bingo!
A crackhead knows how to open closed stores
So you reach back
Like Sosa
Then let go
With a bling-ling-ling
Glass hits the floor
You go, boy!
Just went from crackhead to crack pro
Time to get paid, nigga
You ain't know?
Once inside
You about to quench your thirst
But shit's about to get worse
'Cause you're a brand new thug
And you ain't got no gloves
And your sweaty palms
Have oily prints
That stick to surfaces
Every print is a one-of-a-kind curse
To be found later
And there's a camera, too
The shop-keep recognizes you
As a customer who usually buys Chore Boy and a glass
He stares in shock
Watching in slow-mo as you smash and grab
What the fuck, he asks
Plus Mohammed's got a .44 mag
If he sees you in the streets
Unsteady – with rhythms that would peak an EKG
He'll put a hot one in your ass

POOR RIGHTEOUS POET

For taking his lottery tickets and cigarette packs
You fuckin nerd
Didn't you go to school every day?
Make mostly A's?
Graduate with a taste of success in your mouth
Went to college all bright-eyed and bushy-tailed
Too damned smart to fuck with drugs
Thug with thugs
Way too bright to seek the truth
In the eyes of coke-tooting prostitutes
Damn, dude
Went from too cool to damned fool
To stuffing dope in a tube
How'd this shit happen to you?
Later
When your sober mind rightfully curses you as a clown
You see yourself
Putting the lottery tickets down
Back over the counter you go in one backwards bound
And all the tiny bits of glass
(Even the ones in your shoe)
Fly backwards through the air – pursuing you
The hammer blow somehow unites them
As you swing in a backwards arc
When the tape stops – everything fits
But no matter how much you want this ending to stick
It doesn't fit
You did that shit
You needed a fix and got you a hit!
Ain't no mental trick gonna make it go away
All you can do now is pray
Wait for the police

Wait for sun to beckon day
Wait for the meanest nigga you ever seen
To flirt with you in prison
Treat you like a real queen
You're committing felonies now, dog
Time to get you off the streets
Welcome to the BIG LEAGUE!

Soiled Doves

Arm swinging, the motive is obvious to those
Who indulge in this science, wild nights with wild souls
Despite crow's feet, the wages of age in their eyes
Death rattles, the stages of sin, dark demise
Expectations, brief encounters, unrighteous filled
Sweet temptations, bitter still, sick demons, sicker still
Bitter pills quickly swallowed, detached pleasure, the taste
Liquor spills, flagrant pounding, priceless diamonds decay
Not quite rape; they're submissive to pain, constant drilling
The sick feeling leaves when they meet those who are dealing

My Sorry for 2004

I'm sorry for 2004
2002 and '3 were war
I tried and cried and whored my pride
I shamed my family and the Lord

In discontent, reality bent
I spent my soul on worthless dreams
The trials, the strife, the worthless nights

POOR RIGHTEOUS POET

My life; a periled, stormy stream

But what to do? Beat black and blue
I knew repentance time was due
Yet still I thugged. A stick in the mud
I scorned my wife and children, too

As I drowned, my family frowned
My homies clowned, my head kept down
I lost my things, my home, my dreams
My life, my being, pound after pound

Finally my eyes were dimmed and I
Thought suicide would make things right
But if I did, my mom, my kids
Would never see me change my life

But finally a place for me
On bended knees, I voice my pleas
And by degrees, I'm slowly freed
And I can breathe. Thank God, I'm free!

I'm sorry for 2004
I beg the Lord and my adored
To be forgiven, and know I'm driven
To make amends forever more

Da Crack Poem

First of all
Let's get this straight off the bat

I got a pocket full of crack
Let that be known 'cause this ain't no fuckin riddle
Like the Pied Piper or the cat and the fiddle
My rats play they own fiddles
I'm just the nigga in the middle
Now, if it's weed you need
You ain't mine yet, G
Go see them Crips on Avenue C
They gots that *stick-icky green*
If that's all you need
Or take your jittery ass to East Side Steve
For Ice
Or meet Yesenia for speed
But when you graduate
And those narcotics ain't enough
You know you need a bigger rush than that sticky stuff
And gradually you can't catch a drain from snorting geek
You come see me
Your new fix is *crack*
Your new name's dopefiend
All along I been having what you need
One good hit
Man, trust me – that's it
I'm taking your ass and teeth out the mix
Your mouth gon' fill up with spit
You gon' take a shit
Fidget and fit
Get on your hands and knees and pick
For tiny bits you dropped
Knowing none of it's that good shit
The hard white and yellow gift you got from me
That's a common skitz

POOR RIGHTEOUS POET

Some hear sirens
Checking windows quick
Barricade the door
Light a cig
Scratch and itch
Beat your kids
Expose your tits
Give Fido a swift hard kick
I'm outta crack, but you still got Kibbles and Bits?
Motherfuck that shit!
Bet not eat quick
'Cause next shopping trip
Dog food ain't on the list
You might cuss and slap your man
The moment he walks in
'Cause he had the nerve to come home with a grin
That's all the proof you need
That he fucked your best friend Kim
And when you slip into these midst
I'll see the shift
Then you my bitch
Ol' crackhead bitch
Yeah, I called you a bitch
Watch you flinch and shiver
Got a dick? Still ain't a man
You's a bitch ass nigga
You know dimes costs ten
You six bits short, miss
And since I don't do fronts
And your ass ain't rich
You can't afford the next hit
It's time to hit a lick

That's right
There's money out there, kid
Turn a trick
Sell your clit
Run out of Walmart with some shit
Wanna go legit? Make a porno flick
They pay three G's
Just be good on your knees
Still short?
Break and enter time, dog. They rich
They got insurance, and they won't miss
Those big screens and stereos
Pricey Polo's
Big money – big money's in grand theft autos
But you better stay solo
'Cause your crackhead friends will snitch
One fifth of my customers get a fat chili brick
And chuck a Nolan Ryan pitch
Those windows won't hold
Bingo!
Crackheads know how to open closed sto's
Grab lottery tickets
Free cartons of cigs
Marlboros and Newports
And when your pay is legit
Come see me with them ends
KNOCK–KNOCK
What's up, nigga? You got paper to spend?
What's that? Hell yea! Big face Ben!
'Bout time, kinfolk. Come on in
KNOCK–KNOCK
Hold up. Yo, who that is?

Damn, girl. I ain't seen you in a bit
You only got eight bucks for that fuck?
Well, *eight is enough*
C'mon, bitch
Get this hit

Backsliding Brothers

Holy hands rise like halos adorning
Bright faces, bright eyes – five o'clock in the morning
Holy Spirit, like dew in the morning rests
In this place, these disciples, worshippers blessed
These men, ex-addicts, convicted felons, the lot
They're shifty, suspicious, double-minded, if not
For the grace of the Lord and the way He adores
This place, the way these men bow down before
His face. If not for His love, so amazing
Their souls would be eternally consumed – blazing
But sometimes the night air ushers small whispers
Like whiskers, they brush at the listeners. Still pictures
Of past times are consuming. They devour the peace
Of their prayers. Hypothermic needles entreat
Much like crack, alcohol, the distant musk of wild whores
Like the Pied Piper calling, bishops sneak past the doors

Addiction

SHOCKING! Drastic, amazing phenomena
Awesome: These spastic cravings for trauma
Wonderfully delicious morsels, like gumdrops
Like raindrops – this train slows not – no stopping

It now. Open the floodgates. It's rolling
This loathing for insipid pleasure, it's growing
It's glowing, consuming like fire, cascading
Downhill – freestyle rollerblading. This blazing
This craving, these wants, this prickling desire
Inspires the masses to die or get higher

Big H

Certain delusions at the ready
Equipped with queer confusion, steady
Goes it – pricking needles flow with
Wonder, Satan's satin. Golden
Sunsets swim like twilights dripping
Illusions of stars and cosmos shifting
Drifting, far, yet further. Listen
Burning sparks like flashbulbs glisten
Fission, shards of diamonds twisted
Gleam, the screams of distant misfits
Echo through time and space, peaking
Heartbeats signal life retreating

Whispers

Be not fooled by the eyes, nor the lips, for the whispers
Softly slither like serpents, seducing sprite listeners
Reducing life flickers like back drafts deprived
Of fuel, precious breaths. Souls in-tuned to the lies
Are seduced, soon consumed by these demons – know legions
Await foolish counsel. Beasts like Satan are scheming

They're teaming with loathing. Anger-filled – for your life
Is a slap in the face. Guard your soul, child. Think twice
Nay, think thrice, for those eyes beckon death to the listeners
Captivated by the fervor of passion-filled whispers

Missing Babies
(A Father's Day poem from skid row)

Missing babies
Who aren't babies anymore
On this day
This day when fathers here and abroad
Wake to hugs
And gifts and Hallmark cards
Ugly ties and blackened toast
And warm regards
I do not
Instead the scars
Are opened and salted
My wife, my children long departed
Their whereabouts unknown
Their safety unconfirmed
Agony burns like a hot brand
Like lemon juice in the eyes
Stinging and awful
Seen by all
Recollections of my fall
Are waterfalls of grief and disgrace and pain
My children
Do they call him *Daddy* or by his first name?
Does he treat them well

Or beat the hell out of them?
This prickly dream
Has nightmarish implications
And I'm unable to call
Unable to vent
This bubbling frustration
I've been humble
I've been complacent
I've been patient
I've been brainwashed
My heart re-wired to feel no sorrow
But days like this
When the full magnitude of my folly
Is forefront
Materialized and palpable
The tears sting my eyes
As I think about my little ones
How long, God
Must I wait
For Dorian?
For Jasmine?
Dear Lord
How long?

He Has Them

Shall Dorian say *Daddy* or *Roland*? This name game's
Like hatred, acidic, impaling. The same thing
I feared as our tension-filled fights escalated
Is here – and now Jasmine's with him, and I hate it
And I made it myself. This predicament's leaning

Towards fate. Pimped-out, prostituted, demeaning
I'm dreaming. There's no way she's with him. My babies
Are not being raised by another. Or maybe
I've fallen, and this vision is truly my destiny
I'm stalling, not wanting to see that she left me
And kept me so far from my offspring. My Jasmine
My Dorian, they're gone from my sight, and I hate it

Dream

Shall insults flow forth wild and free?
And then we'll box, or should I squeeze
Off six quick shots. Frankly I need
Your blood, man. I want you to bleed
Please tell me, does she meet your needs?
My wife's breasts, do you caress each?
Her soft lips, do they speak of me
Or kiss your private places? Dream
Of darkness, deadly shadows. Dream
Of fury, keen and focused. Streams
Of terror that bombard your dreams

For Mama

Gracious and dear, consistently loving
Pillar of wisdom, comforting – nothing
Stands test, nor time, nor pain or fire
As does your love. How I desire
Simply to rise – from this dust, this lowly
Life I live and stand, and slowly
Lift my head and see you smile

Your eyes now gleaming at your child

The Overdose

Crisscrossed convulsions cause confusion to cesarean creatures
Flunkies' flagrant floundering, formally functions as phenomenal features
Bystanders watch wide-eyed. Wistful women wail and scream
Doubters deny he's dying. Distraught demons think it's a dream
Jaundiced janky bodies jerking eerily, just like jazz
Pants pissed, in peculiar positions, from poisonous potions taken fast
Desperate demented dope heads dive head-first towards a daunting death
Nearby nitwits remove the needle, needlessly. He'll take no further breaths

PART FOUR

A
HIGHER
POWER

I Adore You

Come be with me. Live in me. Child, I adore you
I've prepared a good place for you. Know that before you
Was nothing. I longed for your presence. You're created
To love me as I dwell in you, saturated
With joy, perfect peace, faithful love. My beloved
You're mine. I am the truth and the light. My son was it
Not for you that I laid down my life, took your sins
Raised your burdens as I raised the cross, took you in
Made you whole, made you know that I am the true vine
Sweet divine, saved your soul, brought it closer to mine
I'm the rock. I hold heaven's doors open for you
Come be with me. Live in me, child. I adore you

God's Response to Job

Where were you when I formed the earth?
The axis, land and water birthed
The mountains – beckoned wind and storm
Each creature – tell me, did you form
The eagle with your hands? Did you
Breathe life in man? Is this your dew
That gently rests? Each precious life
Molded by you? The days and nights
Are yours? My child, are not these things
My gifts? You dare question your King?
I owe you nothing, yet you please
Me, child. I give you everything

Enemy's Camp

Drop out! These drop-out boys fall out
Like ants out of a mound. Fall out!
The enemy's camp is hit! Lit up!
Give us back what you stole! Drop out!
My life, my things, my dreams – drop out!
At church, God told me to man up!
Scabbed up, Jesus helped me stand up!
The van's full, get in back. We strapped!
We rolling with the Lamb. Give back
My life, my dignity! Take that!
And that! Tuck tail and flee! Pimp-slapped!
Got Satan on his knees! Drop out!
Give me back what you stole! Drop out!

POOR RIGHTEOUS POET

Before I Lay me Down to Sleep

Before I lay me down to sleep
And random snap-shot dreams entreat
As slumber holds. Before I sleep
I pray the Lord my soul to keep

If I should die before I wake
Before dawn comes, if I should take
My last breath. Should I not awake
I pray the Lord my soul to take

Thank you Lord for loving me
Amazing Grace, so great, so sweet
So meek, with humbled heart I seek
Your face, as I lay down to sleep

Drizzles

Shame-faced angels
Black-faced misery
Bloated regrets, rank regards
Thunder relieves pain
Stained and decayed
Strained and filleted
My soul is wide open
Broken from abuse
On this day
Rain keeps falling – dreary drizzles
Pickled in a jar of iniquity
Epistles say He can save my soul – how prickly

These thorns that hold me, ensnare me
Like missiles
Like warheads bombarding my psyche
This might be my last chance for salvation
This Bible
Unlikely He'll like me
He'll see me unworthy
Unnerving – this hurting
These choices, these gospels
Is this my end?
This friend
Heaven sent
Takes my hand
Takes me in
It begins

Loneliness

Depressed thoughts turn to suicide
Devoid of laughter, now void of pride
No dark valley's deep enough to hide
The true depths of my loneliness

Mother Nature offers wet and gloomy
Darkened forecasts threaten to doom me
My pity party is dark and roomy
I'm blanketed in loneliness

As the night steals light from day
And shadows creep and stretch my way
On bended knees, head down, I pray

Lord, free me from my loneliness

Matthew 6:6

Silence, mild darkness – timid peace only broken
By voices, screaming some. Potent prayers aptly spoken
Craftsmen broken as their dreams quaver still out of reach
Counsel failed, like the nails meant to silence their King
On their knees, bitter pills, bitter still, for the taste
Of demise, sprinkled lies. They cry out from the waste
Lowered faces – disgraced pain, gruesome longing. How Lord
Did it get so far warped? Regrets pound and distort
Perfect joy – vision blurs. Through exhaustion they seek
To be washed clean of sin by the blood of their King

Be Lord

Be Lord, be universe, be water, be fire
Be perfect, be bread of my life. I desire
Your presence, much more of your glory, your grace
Your mercy. But I am unworthy. Please replace
Imperfections. Make my heart like yours, Lord. I pray
For your presence, for healing, for comfort, I pray

Burdens Down

I brought the Lord my hopes, my dreams
My fears, my tears – those secret things
That had me bound by sin, those schemes

That had me crowned by Satan. Clean
My heart, my mind, my soul. I prayed
For peace, for sweet relief. I gave
Up things that did not please Him. Left
My burdens at the altar, wept
With joy: The Holy Spirit glowed
About me. On my knees, my soul
Was lifted to a higher place
My sins forgiven by His grace

Lamb of God

Take this bread
This is my body
Given for you
Whipped and abused
Beat and battered
Pierced and shattered
Nailed fully through
This is my body
Given for you
Take this cup
This is my blood
That has been spilled
On Calvary
Remember this
As it's consumed
Given for you
My sacrifice
The Lamb of God
Laid down His life

Let it Rain
(A Spiritual rap)

Sometimes the darkness be stalking
Up out of my bed, I'm sleep walking
Cries filled with dread, just like my life
But I keep my head up regardless
'Cause the enemy's looking to make me backslide
If I slip in this water
The enemy's looking to take my head off
If I'm weak in this slaughter
So I gotta keep holding on
Gotta find hope when hope is gone
Gotta keep pressing on
When I feel like I'm slipping from my Savior's throne
'Cause if I'm weak, then I'm leaving
Can't turn my back on these legions
Can't catch my breath, but I'm breathing
I gotta break loose from these demons
Up outta my darkness, there's freedom
He's taking the pain out, believe Him
I'm running from hell, my homies bailing
But it don't matter, don't need 'em
Please forgive me, Lord
And take away my darkest pain
I feel it
Lift my spirits
Let the floodgates loose on me
And let it rain!

Acid Rain

My eyes deserve to well with tears
Memories of my sins appear
Like flashbulbs burning deep within
My soul. Accusing. No pretense
Abusing. Now the acid rain
Stains blissful memories. The pain's
Like solemn melodies. My heart
Clings fast to fleeting dreams. Depart
From me – this bitter sting. Be gone!
Regrets, this stress, this somber song
Relief is mine. In Him I claim
Peace, shelter from this acid rain

Romans 7 & 8

Lord, why am I so wretched?
Knowing the wages of sin is death, yet
My soul is surrounded by flesh
Messy and wicked, with every breath
Sadly, I know what not to do
I know the word of God is true
Still, sin conquers me in the end
My physical being is a slave to sin
Why do I do the evil I hate?
Why has my flesh bound me as a slave
Living as who I'd rather not be?
This conflict that dwells within me
Makes me woeful, but there's a light
In the Spirit, I'm offered new life

POOR RIGHTEOUS POET

No longer captive: Exalted! I'm free
Life is given to those who believe

Trapped
(A Spiritual rap)

I'm trapped
Up in this warzone, fighting the enemy every day
You feeling me?
I got my sword, I got my shield
But still he keeps on drilling me
I'm falling to my knees, my fists are in the air
Saying please send your grace down
Listen to this sinner's prayer
I'm hopeless
I gotta stay focused on the lines
Every single grain of sand dripping through this hour glass
Lord, you know I'm just a man
And I'm running out of time
I'm trying!
You demand that I give worship
If I do, I know it'll be worth it
Help me
Lord, help me get away
I'm trying
To live your way
I'm crying
'Cause every day I'm dying
If you feel me, Jesus, pick up the pieces
Don't just leave us
We at the mountain, and we're hungry

Pass the baskets and feed us

Demons: My Testimony

When I was little, I didn't believe in demons
And that's strange, because my favorite author at the time
Was Stephen King
And I was only twelve or thirteen
And sometimes I couldn't sleep because of the things I read
The most ghoulish creatures imaginable
Would chase me in my dreams
But I knew that was make-believe
And they could never really harm me
When I was thirteen

When I was sixteen
My brother started to hang in the streets
And he wore his pants low
And his hair long
And he had a crew that smoked weed
And snorted 'caine
And talked in slang
And twisted up their fingers when they repped their gang
And sometimes
I got caught up when those guns went BANG!
And I even got shot in the head one time
But I still didn't see demons
Just Negroes behaving badly
It got wild on those streets
But still, it wasn't that deep

POOR RIGHTEOUS POET

I think I finally opened my eyes when I was twenty-seven
That's when all of my bad deeds started to simmer
And bubble over
And that's when my wife told me it was over
And all of the pain and regret was like a two-ton boulder
And I couldn't bear the weight
At least not while I was sober
And the green leaves in my cigar
Made my empty home a little less lonely
And as a substitute for my children
I had the warm embrace of hard liquor to hold me
And the whore hanging at the corner store
Was more than eager to come home with me
She asked if it was alright if she smoked some 'caine
I told her *Yeah, girl. Do your thing*

The next few years
Almost a blur
It was then that saw demons
Sick and spooky
Fish-eyed and drooling
Hell-bound and loving it
Countless legions
Stuck in sin
Eyes wide shut
In high definition
I saw demons
And they were intriguing
Beautiful even
I lived among them
Inhaled their essence
I lost so much

Everything I had
I watched it all go
Through my foggy spectacles
And bloodshot eyes

I was living on the streets
When He found me
Took my hand
Brought me inside
Gave me food and shelter and clothing
Gave me the Word that change my life
In return, He only asked me to believe
That His only begotten son
Gave His life
For me

Since then
I don't talk much about where I've been
My only focus is where I'm going
But there's not a day that I don't give thanks
There's not a day that I don't show Him
That I'm a devoted father now
A passionate worker
Constantly setting and obtaining my goals
Constantly shining His light through me
And if I can only reach *one* soul
I'm obligated to tell him
That I'VE BEEN THERE
I was a thief, a tramp, a vagabond, a fiend
But by the grace of God, I'm NO LONGER THERE
And He loves you, too
He's everything you need

PART FIVE

STOP!
THE VIOLENCE

I'll Take Your Blood

In Africa
I wasn't there
When strong black men sliced through their dark skin
With sharp blades
And they sang
And they danced
And their thick, pure blood flowed freely from their bodies
Into the pure African soil
I wasn't there
So
I waited
In America, I'm at almost every street corner
With my big cement mouth open wide
And I gobble up skateboards and garbage
Children's toys and leaves
And you

When you roll down the streets
With those colored handkerchiefs on your head
I see you
And I wait
And when they come for you
With bigger guns than yours
And when their hot pieces of lead enter your body
You will bleed
And your thick, pure blood
Will flow freely from your body
Onto these oil-streaked American streets
And I'll take your blood
And taste it
And let it stain my insides
Until the rain comes
And your thick, pure blood will be washed away
With all of the skateboards and garbage
Children's toys and leaves
And all other human waste

A Bullet and a Knuckle

Hi
I'm a knuckle
Don't mess with me
Especially while I'm balled up in this fist
About to give you a bloody nose
Alright
Go ahead and crack jokes
You ain't feeling me
That's cool

POOR RIGHTEOUS POET

I know it's not my time anymore
I've been pretty much forgotten nowadays
But man, I used to be the shit
Back in the day, boy, I was getting some serious action
I'm talking 'bout some straight knuckling up
I remember when I'd get the chance to bust a lip
Or swell a jaw
What? Thought you knew!
I remember this one time
When I actually knocked out a *tooth*!
I did that!
Man, I was the bomb
It's like, those were the days, ya know?
But now
Dang, now everything has changed
People forget they even have knuckles
You only think about us when you bang or scrape us
While you're doing plumbing jobs
Or working on your cars
By the way, could y'all please try to be more careful?
Nowadays, ain't nobody hitting nobody
It's just shoot em up, bang-bang all the time
Don't take no skill for that
That's alright, though
It's cool
'Cause you know what
I'm making a comeback
I can feel it
One day
I'll be back on top

What up?

I'm a hollow-tipped .45 caliber slug
Bitch, don't fuck with me
Especially while I'm chilling in this weapon
Waiting for the firing pin to set me off
I'm hoping you'll do something stupid, like take off running
Keep talking that noise
You know, keep bumping that
Nigga, I don't give a fuck about yo gun, shit
'Cause I want you bad
So very bad
Fuck busting a nose
I wanna bust through your sternum
Blaze my way through your muscles and tissue
Tear through that tough-man heart of yours
And leave a big-ass hole the size of a fist
On my way out your back
Ya punk
You ain't so tough now, is ya?
You ain't so bad now
Breathing through a hole in your chest
Bubbling at the lips
I'll have you coughing up piss and blood
Have you wearing a colostomy bag
Have you running down the street screaming
I'm on fire!
I'm on fire!
And you is, you ho
Your skin got 2nd and 3rd degree burns
Nick you in the face, and you gon' look jacked up for life
And that's *if* you live
I'm chilling
Waiting for an offense

You trying to steal my man's car?
BAM!
What? You wanna pull knives and shit?
BAM!
I know you ain't sleeping with my man's wife
Oh boy!
Say it ain't so!
Now I'm peeping you – both of you
Through this barrel of this gun
I'm looking you dead in the eyes
Y'all both bucky-nekkid
Ooooh weeee!
I'm bouncing with anticipation
Please say something slick
Get aggressive, fool!
C'mon
C'mon!
Pull the trigger, dog
Let me at em

Colored Rags

The gutters take your blood and bile
These gangstas with those sinful smiles
With colored rags spread country miles
Tec-9 is Dad to the bastard child
And so a grin streaks your face while
The bullets buck from kids gone wild

And then you spoil the walls with paint
When your locs meet their futile fate

Of bars that are their pearly gates
Or muddy holes where fat worms mate
Hospital beds where flat lines skate
Morticians drive nice cars and wait

For customers when handguns blast
For gangstas with those grinning masks
For you to cock yo fo' fo' mags
And smoke some leaves, then start to laugh
And give your nose a crystal bath
Then pump some lead in his bitch ass!
Yeeeah!
I guess you got revenge at last
Our caps get pealed for colored rags

Dulce et Decorum
(Tribute to Wilfred Owen)

Small infractions could draw the line
Between life and death – the living and the dead
Last time they missed, but you're bleeding this time
Bits of tooth and moustache blown from your head

Black pride and brown pride sound good on TV
It's a rhetoric that fills us with simplistic joy
But pride is only shown when you uplift your street
Your clique was unified in stomping that boy

Explosions taunt every weekend night
What started as an argument ends in gunplay
Slugs quickly pursue those who flee in fright

POOR RIGHTEOUS POET

God's mercy leaves the hapless merely grazed

Who's that? Say, watch out! is the only warning
Lowered windows spit fire as a Cutlass cruised
An ecstasy of fumbling, fire and bullets swarming
One is caught, stunned and bloodied, grotesquely misused

If you could see the bloodshot eyes
Of this youngster – body torn – inexplicably gory
You would not tell the next gangster that same old lie
*Dulce et decorum est, pro patria mori

*Latin: It is sweet and fitting to die for one's country

A Place for Me

I cussed and punked my teacher. Check it – I'm too cool
Principal straight up told me, *Boy, get out my school*!
So it's they fault if I don't graduate
Them fools, what – they expected me to beg to stay?
And it's also they fault I can't read
School damn sure wasn't the place for me

School's out, for me at least, so I kick with a gang
Niggas call me Lil Hoova, where I hang
It's cool, 'til somebody stole my OG's weed
Since I'm a Baby Gangsta, them fools blamed me
They skinned me up and kicked me off my own street
Through tears, I'm looking for a place for me

Rumors spread, I got heart, so Mike fronted me some rocks

I got nuts, so I slang 'em right on my block
My old homies jacked me up and whooped me good
Now Mike's pissed, he pistol gripping, 'cause I lost his goods
I'm fucked up. They think I'm soft, 'cause I'm just 16
But I be knowing, and I'm formulating a place for me

I got a gat for three dimes, from old school Pops
I smoked one of them niggas that jacked my rocks
I rolled by Mike's crib, steady blazing my gun
I let some off at my high school, just for fun
Them police wasn't playing – put me six feet deep
Bingo, them hoes found a place for me

Badass

Booming firearms like canons
Shake the life from foes. Abandoned
Bodies free of souls, transfixed
With burning, gaping holes betwixt
Their eyes, mowed down for small infractions
Big badass sat down for actin'
Tougher than the ones with pistols
The *cha-chick* of guns cocked is crystal
Clear to hoodlums in the know
Split-seconds count. Chin-check the flo'
Bum-rush the do', lest medics find
Your big bad ass stuck out of time

POOR RIGHTEOUS POET

Drip Drop

Damn, homey
You alright?
You got hit, do you remember?
Remember how you was talking noise
To them hardheads in that car
Then you saw a gun sticking out of the window
You remember how you started running
And you *almost* got away
And then you felt something like a sledgehammer
Slam into your back
And you fell down
And felt your blood dripping from your body
Drip drop

Say, kid
You alright?
They got you at the hospital
Trying to get you some help, man
You need some serious healing
Do you remember what happened?
How you got shot?
It looks pretty bad
The doctor say you got hit in the spine
And you probably won't walk again
You might not ever sit up on your own
You remember?
Your mom is here too, man
She looks pretty sad
Oh, by the way, you died last night, homey

You remember?
Your mom is leaning over you
Do you feel her tears
Falling on your face?
Drip drop

Damn, dude
Look where they got you now
It's chilly in here
You got a fresh tag on your toe
They got all kinds of weird knives and saws
They cut your chest and stomach open, in a big Y shape
Do you remember?
They got some tubes stuck in you
Now they're taking out your blood
Replacing it with some, *icky stuff*
This is straight up nasty!
Here comes some of that stuff now
Do you see it?
Drip drop

Damn!
My nigga!
Looking good in your new suit, playa
Got your hair all shiny
But you still look dead, though
Not asleep, like the mortician promised
Your funeral was today, dog
Some of your homeboys were there
None of them cried, though
Do you remember?
You remember how they drove you out to the cemetery

And when they took you out of the hearse
The sky started to rumble
Then, uh-oh, the rain started
Now it's pouring
Everybody's getting back in their cars
They ain't finna mess up their good clothes for this
Your mama still here, though
And the preacher man, you know he can't leave her
Can you hear the rain
Falling on your casket?
Drip drop

Crime Caucuses

Hoodlums find time for folly, constant friction
And addiction. Boy/Girl spots get hit up, cuz, listen
To these demons, street-level crime caucuses meeting
A little death, a few beat-downs. Blast the fleeing. Fuck retreating
Bustas bleeding. Ooh wee mayne! Life is leaving, maggots feeding
Now we even, but ain't no peace in this game, dog. We scheming
Steady dreaming of better days, getting paid, stomach growling
Fine ass broads coochie popping, gotta get laid, steady prowling
Laws can't fix all this shit. Quit bull-shitting. Niggas wild
Get your pistols, filling clips, bullets spraying in the crowd
Every day is payback time. If you scared, get to running
*Find a bag to put the guns in, and come on if you coming

*Notorious B.I.G.

Filthy

It's filthy, my life
I've seen so many crimes
The victims, misused, and the mothers that cried
The dead ones, I see them when I close my eyes
And the way they were drilled on the cold nights they died

POP! POP!
Hot rocks hit my homeboy this time
His soul is at peace, but I still see chalk lines
Another young brother taken out in his prime
And the pain that I feel is corrupting my mind

But it's not just the pain
It's the shame
I brought that nigga in the gang
Now all I got is dark stains
From his blood on my shoe strings
So I'll bang for his name
Until I'm just the same

At the funeral, the rain wets my face as I cry
When they lower his casket to the other side
And I've learned through the years not to ask the Lord why
So I lie when I pray, hope He buys my disguise

Innocent

I think I got hit in the chest
But I'm not totally sure
My whole body wants to rest
From the pain it has endured
I think I felt two bullets drill me
But I don't know who to blame
Why would my people want to kill me?
I'm not even in a gang
Maybe it's because of what I wore
Tonight I *think* I had on red
Is that what he shot me for?
That why he tried to split my head?
And these doctors need to quit
Asking if I can feel my toes
I told them fools I can't feel shit!
And why am I so goddamned cold?
Are you people gonna save me?
Y'all gon' put me back in place?
And what about the fool that sprayed me?
I guess he just gon' get away
And tell me why I feel so cold
How come it's so hard to breathe?
Doctor, please don't let me go
I don't want my mom to grieve
Did he think I was a Blood
Or now is wearing colors enough?
When that fool said, *What's up, cuz?*
I told him, *I ain't in that stuff*
Then my body had new holes

And I was staring at the sky
Please tell me why I feel so cold
Doctor, please don't let me die

The First 48

Flipping through my DVR
Bored as hell
And then I see my show!
The First 48!
My heartbeats quicken as I race to the kitchen
Grab me some summer sausage and cheese
Cool Ranch Doritos
Run back to my favorite recliner
Grab the remote
It's 'bout to go down
This right here is my show!

In the opening segment
They tell me what today's episode is gonna be
It's a double-feature
Two piece!
Except in the first one, it's two murders
So it's really a *three piece*!
And I already know they gon' catch the killer
'Cause they show this dude in handcuffs
That nigga think he tough
He look right at the camera and say
Fuck y'all bitches, this east side for life!
They beep out his curse words
But I know I read his lips right

POOR RIGHTEOUS POET

And I'm on the edge of my seat
'Cause *that's* a motherfucking sound bite!
They play that shit right before the theme music
Then they get into it

The first story's from Harris County, Texas
Two dudes got beat up and shot in a vacant lot
One of them got a pocket full of rocks
So we already know the plot
The next story's from Florida
Liberty City neighborhood, better known as Pork and Beans
A thirteen year old girl got blasted
She laying in the street
They blur most of her body
But they show up to her knees
She ain't have no shoes on her feet
I'm sipping on my soda
Eating summer sausage
Popping Doritos and chunks of cheese
And that dead girl's mama begging the police to
Please, get my baby off the street!

I put that shit on pause
Go to the bathroom
Look in the mirror
And use my toothbrush to get a piece of meat out my teeth
When I get back, that dead girl's mama
Still want her baby off the street
And it's a little part of me that thinks it's wrong
To get entertainment from the deceased
But if somebody wrong, it can't be me
I ain't the one who put this shit on TV

They go back to the first story – the double murder
Them niggas was dope boys
Got caught slipping
But the killers was slipping, too
'Cause all them niggas got caught
And I'm laughing, 'cause these fools be like:
Yes, I understand my rights
I'll answer your questions
Cameras rolling
They start talking
Now the detective got 'em second-guessing
Huh, hold up, sir
I do need a lawyer
'Cause I ain't the one who pulled the trigger!
But you done already told them you was down for the ride
I'm shaking my head at these dumb niggas
And they arrest a second one and a third
Then they arrest one more
Caught the trigger man, got him cuffed on the floor
And right before commercial break
He say what I been waiting for
Fuck y'all bitches, this east side for life!
And I'm so hype, I jump up and drop my summer sausage
Five second rule, this shit's still good
They cut back to the other story
From the Pork and Beans neighborhood

And now I'm bugging
'Cause it was broad daylight when the cops got to that scene
And now it's dark
And I'll be damned

POOR RIGHTEOUS POET

That little girl is *still* lying in the street
Turns out she was innocent
Minding her own business
Her only problem was playing outside
In a bad neighborhood where they do drivebys
And they got more bullets buzzing than a beehive
And when they catch her killer, he don't want a lawyer either
Just started talking
The detective just listened
The killer was remorseful
But he still got sent to prison
And when the show's over
I feel good
Even though I do math very well:
In one episode I saw three people dead
Five people sent to jail
That's a total of EIGHT BLACK PEOPLE GONE
I'm glad it's peaceful in my city
Shit like that don't be going on

But when I go to bed that night
I'm *kinda* tripping
I can't go straight to sleep
'Cause I see that dead girl
Her dusty feet
Her mama pleading to get her baby off the street
Her mama screaming
And I ask myself
Am I wrong
For watching?
For eating?
For laughing?

Nah, can't be
I ain't the one put them fools on TV
To ease my mind, I think of something funny
A moment later my smile lights up the night
That Harris County nigga was dumb as fuck
But he gave them one hell of a sound bite!
Fuck y'all bitches, this east side for life!
Ha ha! That's my motherfucking show!
The First 48 be hella tight!

The Killing Field

It's broad daylight when tires squeal
Forty ounce delusions seem unreal
But yes, those gunshots mean the deal
Is off, and you ain't got no shield
You watch your homeboy's cap get pealed
Fool, welcome to the killing field

Uh oh, these folks is way too tough
You bad, yeah, bad enough to duck
Protect your head, plus guard your guts
'Cause shit bags leave a nigga stuck
You know for sure your set's fucked up
The gunshots stop, and you get up

It's bloody. Damn, how many killed?
Hector, Luis, both bodies filled
With new holes. Jaime too's been drilled
Wide-eyed and crumpled, his hot blood spills
You see ghosts, and you know they're real

POOR RIGHTEOUS POET

Boy, welcome to the killing field

What is Black?

What is black?
Black is the darkness of the heart of the black man
It's the black faces in the Cutlass Supreme
It's the black faces of the rivals on the corner
It's the black hands gesticulating territorial boundaries
It's the black fingers bent on the triggers of the weapons
Black is the color of pupils dilated in fear
Black is the color of smoke after the explosion
It's your black wig split

Black is the color of your mother's mascara as it runs
Black is the color of the dress you make her wear
Black is the color of the used suit you sport
Black is the color of your goatee – finally trimmed neat
Black is what you see when you close your eyes in the shade
Black is what you see when you never open your eyes again
Black is the color of the earth
Six feet deep
Black is the black man
Black is the darkness of the heart of the black man

Put Down Your Guns

Do you prefer a driveby, or do stabbings make you smile?
Are your dreams ever tormented by the screams of an innocent child?

Or is anyone worthy of innocence in your quest for ghetto fame?
Do you feel a twinge of guilt for any bloodied corpse left slain?
This genocide has gone on for years, isn't it getting kinda old?
Brothers, put down your guns. You still have time to save your souls

Our people are being wiped out by the nine millimeter disease
But still the hot rocks fly. We preach mo' murda over a street
They'll spray your name on someone's wall for getting took out of the game
And your homeys will pour out liquor six feet above your lost remains
Your mom bought an air-tight casket – but worms have forever, they'll get in
Brothers, put down your guns. The prisons have too much black skin

You check him at the club – just words, but words lead to gunplay
He's pissed, and this dude's deep, so now he's looking for where you stay
His boys wet up your brother, 'cause you're always on the run
This ain't the 60's, fool. You thought they'd keep it one-on-one?
Do you think your brother knew it was your fault he faced their guns?

Now you gotta tell your mama how you killed her youngest son
Bet you didn't feel so bad when it was someone else's kid
Brothers, put down your guns. You're making Gregory Spencer rich

You don't even stick around to watch your target hit the street
To see his body jerk and spasm, piss himself as his life leaves
You don't inspect your fallen prey! You don't watch that black man bleed!
You don't watch his last breath form as a spit bubble between his teeth
You don't stay until he's stiff, until your adversary turns cold
Brothers, put down your guns. Please try to save your wicked souls

Mansfield County Jail

You better have your Nikes on
'Cause these youngsters are out for blood
Bored and frustrated
Charges upgraded to aggravated
And this one in particular
Has been on the phone all day, but can't make bail
And he hates it
And he can't be faded
Bobbing and weaving
Cassius Clay'ing
His problems are in the free-world
But somebody in this jail gots to pay

He spots his prey and
Two-pieces him real quick
That's it
Pull the shades down on the simp
Lights out
Chin on his chest
Hulled the fuck out
And while the kid's dancing
The defeated man shit his pants and
He rolls over two hours later
Tasting his blood
Head jamming
Wondering what the hell happened
How the fuck did my forehead
Get this crater?
They tell him he slipped on a tomater
Don't like it, chump?
Bond out!

All for Me

There's death and destruction on my bad streets
The shotgun reports start to sound like bombs
Every weekend leaves more mothers grieved
Daily it sounds like Vietnam

Old school Cutlasses are smooth and mean
When their windows spit, our bodies are lifted
Sometimes slugs go through smooth and clean
We still throw signs with missing digits

Sometimes I contemplate the gang
If I changed my ways and dropped the slang
Would all my enemies do the same?
Would they still claim? Will they still bang?

These questions bring on troubled sleep
I cock my piece with skillful ease
So I'll keep hanging on these streets
Until the grief is all for me

Black Hate

Hot lead discombobulates heads on the weekend
When the week ends for weakened foot soldiers, blood seeping
In shrouds, dark phantoms survey the corpses
When the soul is divorced from the body. This remorseless
Mass murder is like lightening. It's exciting! It's ferocious!
Nail-biting, edge-of-your-seat violence, keen and focused
Like locust laying waste to the land, grinning shooters
Blast first. They blast worst, leaving bile in the sewers
Doing dirt, they do worse than the Klan did. They hate
And they hate their own kind. Foul and putrid decay

Stick in the Mud

Even tough niggas get drove and drug
Beat down, face down, stretched in the mud
For nothing but a *What's up, cuz?*
And you're a Blood, and ain't no love
For games these bustas trying to play

You strapped, you down, down for gunplay
You deep, and bound to get a piece
No peace 'til y'all control the streets
This thang, it's strange, this ghetto gang
This set we claim, this dope we slang
This place were hoodlums know your name
Like *Cheers*, except this kind of fame
Is sick. It's hard to coexist
Your foes fill clips, and when you slip
That's it, you blasted, face in the mud
'Cause even tough niggas get drove and drug

Can't Stop Won't Stop

Fallen foot soldiers get fucked up
Touched up – laid out in ditches
Tucked up with pissy britches
Bucked up 'cause shiesty bitches
Cause ruin for many men
Many, many, many men
Piss bags, sporting Depends
Spinal cords get severed when
Hot rocks fly, perforating
Flesh and skin – decorating
The streets with blood, slick and sticky
Sick and twisty. Mediating
On this mess gives me a migraine
These missing brains and shitty stains
All these remains, glazed and strained
Filleted, displayed in slashing rain
Why should we love when we can hate?

POOR RIGHTEOUS POET

Why build her up when we can rape?
Why should we ask when we can take?
Clear 'em out and clean the slate
This is the life we choose to live
Can't stop it now, this train is rolling
This train is going, faster now
Spitting sparks. This bitch is stolen!

PART SIX

IT'S OKAY TO LAUGH

Lately

Frankly, my decadent darling
The trumpet blast sound of your farting
Shatters the façade of dainty
Princess you portray so quaintly
And I'll be honest, Ma'am, your belching
Smells of bygone meals. It's melting
Paint clean off the walls – vibrating
Furniture, my home is shaking
From the sound. And dear, your spitting
Is grotesque. Once I was smitten
By your charm and grace, but lately
I've found that you are no lady

Dope Ray Me
(Inspired by Do-Re-Mi show tune)

Dope – A drug. It's crack cocaine!
Ray – The guy I got it from
Me – The fiend – the lost dope fiend
Fa – How fa' I had to come
So – I take it to the head
La – I la' down on the flo'
The T – So now I take the bus*
And it takes me back to dope!

*ial*The T* is the public transport system (city bus) in my hometown

Menace in the Sky

If I could soar
Like a bird
Or fly like a kite
I'd be a dysfunctional bee
High above the trees and power lines
I'd be
And I'd gloat
I'd yell down at the masses below
Look at me!
You fools!
You Earthbound clowns!
Look at me!
I can fly!
I'd hover
Above the thieves and adulterers and murderers

And like Superman, I'd watch crimes go down
But unlike Superman, I'd stand idly by
And call the police with conflicting descriptions
And bad license plate information
So that the guilty could flee
And be free
I'd become a prince of thieves
Like Robin Hood, I'd be
Except I'd do no good
And I'd go
Where no man can go
Right up to a bubbling volcano
I'd fly down Niagara Falls
With no barrel or any craft at all
They'd be shocked, stunned, appalled
I'd fly
And I'd catch eagles in mid-glide
And pluck their tail feathers
And make environmentalists cry
I'd be a jinx in the sky
Way up high – higher than God wanted me to be
Right up to heaven, I'd go
I'd tell the angels
Check it out!
You're not so special!
And God would look on
And He would say that I was a menace
A bolt of lightning would strike me down
And I'd plummet to the ground
From which I came
They would build a tomb for me:
Here lies

POOR RIGHTEOUS POET

A hell of a guy
Got too big for his britches
When he learned how to fly

The Killer's Knife

(Inspired by The Facts of Life theme song)

You take the less protected path
The alleyway, and there you have
The killer's knife!
The killer's knife!
There's a time you gotta leave the earth
You're gonna bleed – it's gonna hurt
The killer's knife!
The killer's knife!
Just one slice, and then you'll see
As you're hold-ing on to your spleen
And as you flee, you're gonna see
The killer's knife still coming for – coming for you!
You-ou-ou-ou-ou!
Co-ming for you!
You'd better pro-tect your windpipe
When you're dodging the killer's knife!

Possum

Possum in my room, exactly
Horrible – matter-of-factly
Dark and spooky eyes that shine and
Seek a foot or leg to climb and
Use his claws and razor teeth and

He might have rabies, and he can
Fold up if you grab his tail
Then climb your arm and bite like hell
And hold tight as you try to shake
Him free. A possum might just take
Your finger as a souvenir
This vicious rat warrants all fear!
So back away, for now, withhold
Bravado and call pest control

Different Chokes
(Inspired by Different Strokes theme song)

All windpipes don't bruise
To the squeeze of just one choke
What cuts the air from Sue
May not kill other folk
A man is strong!
With big hands and means
Those big hands on you
Will surely cut short your screams
But it takes – different chokes
It takes different chokes
It takes different chokes to kill your girl
Now everybody's got a different killing technique
Extension cords is yours, headlocks is mine!
Some guys choke her in the tub
Rub-a-dub!
Or with a noose, or duct tape or you can choke her from behind
And don't stop if she starts crying!

'Cause it takes different chokes to kill your girl
Yes it does
It takes different chokes to kill your girl!

These Bars

Man, I done had the finest women
Done drove the baddest cars
From the hoods of New York to the dirty South
Niggas know that I went hard
I was pushing more than five ki's a week
Had bank accounts and credit cards
But I'd give up all that shit I had
To get away from these goddamned bars!

They didn't give the jury no evidence
The D.A. was a straight up mark!
A few busters plea-bargained and testified against me
You know snitches ain't got no heart
They ain't find no 'caine, not one crumb of crack
Just a couple of paid-for remarks
Then that fat, black robe wearing sonofabitch
Put my ass behind these goddamned bars!

Nigga, I done been so many places
In Hollywood, I was kicking it with stars
I got a Benz, a Porsche, all kinds of bling
A pretty nigga, manicured, no scars
Bought my mama a house, the pastor got a new church
People love me like Escobar
But I'd trade all that for one helicopter

To fly me out these goddamned bars!

Texas Hell

Summertime
Texas hell
Frying babies on the sidewalk
The heat index is stalking
The elderly
Who stay home
And scream
With melted ice cream
Dripping from their chin
Thunder clouds are pinned
Between two mighty sunrays
Like a haze of blazing fire
That saps the desire for all outdoor activities
The sand at the lake has become glass
Vehicles leave melted tires in the streets
And the policeman has abandoned his beat
And the thief has passed out
With a knapsack full of liquefied DVD's on his back
And birds die
And squirrels die
And bullfrogs fry in the fields
Covered with flaming lilies
And the Trinity River is but a trickle
And the devil is tickled
And the postman has died
And construction workers die
And the milkman brings yogurt

And then he dies
In Texas

The Poisoned Punch

(Inspired by The Brady Bunch theme song)

It's the story
Of a bunch of crazies
Who were spread out all over the USA
They were weird and looking for a leader
They thought Star Trek was great

It's the story
Of a kooky fellow
Who started a religion he called Heaven's Gate
He thought a comet would bring a big spaceship
To take them all away

'Til the one day when he gathered all these people
And they knew that it was much more than a hunch
That they should all put on purple Nikes
And gulp down a big ol' cup of poisoned punch!

Some poisoned punch!
Some poisoned punch!
And gulp down a big ol' cup of poisoned punch!

If Deer Had Guns

If deer had guns, they'd lie in ambush in the forest, after rolling around in old campfires to disguise their smell. They would wait for the tangy scent of man to catch their attention. They'd set the sights of their rifle in the clearing and hold their breath when a healthy male appeared. Hopefully he'd be wearing an orange vest, to identify he's in season. The deer would squint through the scope for a good kill shot, just to the right of the sternum, and...

If whales had harpoons, they'd search from beneath the ocean for an old whaling ship with barnacles eating away at the bottom of it. The whale would swim out to a safe distance and peek above the surface of the water until it spotted him; an evil-hearted captain with a scope against his eye and a corn pipe nestled between his teeth. The whale would aim the rusting arrow of its harpoon at the captain's belly, just as the captain's binoculars spotted the whale and...

If monkeys had labs, they would strap guinea humans down in metal chairs and hold their eyelids open with clothespins. They would use turkey basters to introduce a various assortment of toxic chemicals into the human eyeballs – not for any beneficial purpose, simply to chart the relationship between human pain and monkey pleasure.

Good thing they're all dumber than us.

If She Delights You

If she delights you, the mere thought
Of her sheer beauty has you caught
Up in a sea of wistful bliss
If you love her, and you miss

Her when she's gone. Her feel, her touch
Is just enough to make you blush
And if you long to hold her hand
And if your heart simply demands
To be with her – to kiss her lips
Caress her neck, her spine, her hips
If she could never be replaced
And you're a girl too, you're probably gay

Those Were the Days
(Inspired by All in the Family theme song)

Boy, the way Glenn Miller played
Back when blacks were kept backstage
Before the coloreds had it made
Those were the days!

Red, white, and blue was purer then
Uptown was filled with real white men
Mister, we could use a man like Gov'ner Wallace again

Separate schools were working great
The Negroes really knew their place
Before they voted J.F.K.
Those were the days!

Snot Dragons

Children smart-off and giggle and fart
And fall from trees and crash go-carts
And stick their fingers in their noses

They'll pull out a booger, roll it and hold it
And stick it on the family couch
(Some weird kids stick them in their mouths)
Children poke fun and run amuck
They fall and cry and sometimes suck
Their thumbs – constantly – regardless of races
And make their parents buy them braces
Children push and shove and shout
They wet their beds, and there's no doubt
They'd go to hell, if they were grown-ups
But since they're young, they're free to shuck
And jive and spit, and they can't sing!
They swear and stink, but here's the thing
We love and want them in our homes
We'd miss them much, if they were gone

Y'all Niggas Tripping

I'm tired of jacked Cutlass cruising, drive-by shooting, good women abusing, jacking youngsters for their shoes, and beating their children black and blue, and good *Showtime at the Apollo* singers booing ass niggas

I'm tired of drug dealing, Cadillac stealing, doughnut pealing, corner store chilling, fake platinum teeth grilling, big booty hoes drilling ass niggas

I'm tired of steady banging in the streets, ain't never trying to hear no peace, selling crack to all the fiends, steady gone off pills and weed, quick to squab if there's a need, ready to blast their enemies ass niggas

I'm tired of step on my sneaker at the club, can't you see that I'm a thug, what you talking 'bout *One love*? I ain't with that black pride stuff, nigga we boxing with no gloves, yo punk ass 'bout to get straight drug ass niggas

I'm tired of yeah I'm pimping both these hoes, what you looking at me fo', beat yo ass down to the flo', send my gals boosting at the sto', if they get caught, I'll get two mo', bitch better have my money, so I can sco' ass niggas

I'm tired of gang banging, dope slanging, on the cut hanging, always talking about they banking, steady grabbing on they thang, and I know you ain't gon' leave me hanging ass niggas

Y'all niggas tripping

You're Black Too

Do you ever wonder why it is that as you're leaving work from your high-rise office building, wearing your power suit, laughing with a few co-workers about a joke you overheard at the water cooler (it was one of those *There was a white man, a black man and a Mexican man* jokes that was abruptly cut off as you approached, but you reassured them that you, in fact, loved those types of jokes, and it wasn't a problem at all– which created a huge sense of relief among your colleagues), do you ever wonder why, as you reach the sidewalk, the homeless black person stops mumbling to himself and looks directly at you? He's filthy and stinky and possibly drunk – with no sense of personal hygiene whatsoever. As you try to walk by, do you wonder why he singles you out of the group with his disgusting intrusion: *Say brotha, do you, can you spare some change?...*

And do you ever wonder why it is that as you continue your walk to the parking garage, and you spot a ghetto youth ahead of you on the sidewalk – walking STRAIGHT TOWARDS YOU – and you see that he has an earring in each ear, and one of those *corn row* hair styles, and you see that the jeans he's wearing are baggy enough to conceal all sorts of weaponry, so you scurry across the street quickly, attempting to look casual as you avoid the possible threat, but in your haste, you almost collide with a small, white woman on the other side of the road. Do you wonder why she gasps and clutches her purse close to her body and backs away from you with wide-eyed fear? What does she have to be afraid of? The GANGSTER you avoided is across the street...

And do you ever wonder why it is that when you finally get home and have a moment to sit back and relax in your easy chair, and your windows begin to rattle with thundering RAP MUSIC from the people next door, and you rise to your feet and scream, *THAT IS IT!* and within a month you've packed up your family and moved all the way across town, to a neighborhood with manicured lawns and pretty street names and year-to-date cars in the driveways. Do you wonder why it is that as you unload your moving truck, and your children play in the front yard, your new neighbor stands in his doorway staring at you, with a look on his face like the stock market just crashed? What is he worried about? You're not like those *other* black people.

POOR RIGHTEOUS POET

Maybe it's because
You're black, too

THE END
BY KEITH THOMAS WALKER

ABOUT THE AUTHOR

Keith Thomas Walker, known as the Master of Romantic Suspense and Urban Fiction, is the author of more than a dozen novels, including *Fixin' Tyrone*, *Dripping Chocolate* and *The Realest Ever*. Keith enjoys reading, poetry and music of all genres. Originally from Fort Worth, he is a graduate of Texas Wesleyan University. Keith was nominated for an Emma Award in 2010 for Debut Author of the Year. In 2012 Keith was the recipient of a BRAB Book Club Award for Male Author of the Year as well as a SORMAG award for Fiction Author of the Year. Visit him at www.keithwalkerbooks.com.

www.ingramcontent.com/pod-product-compliance
Lightning Source LLC
Chambersburg PA
CBHW051454290426
44109CB00016B/1753